Old Men on Tuesday Mornings

Old Men on Tuesday Mornings

Poems

Lyman Grant

ALAMO BAY PRESS
SEADRIFT•AUSTIN

Copyright © 2017 by Lyman Grant

All rights reserved. No part of this book may be reproduced in any form without permission in writing from the publisher, except by a reviewer who may quote brief passages in a review.

Cover Photograph: Mark St. Gil, US National Archives
Book Design: ABP

For orders and information:
Alamo Bay Press
Pamela Booton, Director
825 W 11th Ste 114
Austin, Texas 78701
pam@alamobaypress.com
www.alamobaypress.com

Library of Congress Control Number: 2017947144
ISBN: 978-1-943306-08-4

For

Bill Jeffers
David Jewel
John Lee
John McElhenney

What caused each of us to live hidden?
A wound, the wind, a word, a parent.
   —Robert Bly

We talked about mileage.
   —John Lee

We finally die from the exhaustion of becoming.
   —Jim Harrison

Contents

    Part One

1. Small Bird
2. Humanities
3. So They Say
4. Outer Banks
5. Suspended
6. Fat Man Olympiad
7. Following the News
8. Wandering and Believing
9. Survival Tactic
10. The List
11. Deep End
12. Little Storm
13. Morning Drive
14. Imagining Paradise
15. Ghost Story
16. Seasons
17. Fresher Air
18. From What Planet
19. Cooking

    Part Two

23. Ode American

    Part Three

33. Old Men on Tuesday Mornings
34. Heirlooms
35. With Time

36	Bio
38	At Eighty-Four
39	Lab Work
40	Last Rights for a Family Man
41	Shame and the Silent Moon
42	Clear Steam
43	Hot and Sour
44	Guarding
45	Family Pride
46	Affluence
47	Success
48	Open Carry
50	Waffle House
51	Arroyo Sunset
52	Here They Are
53	Mountain Prayer
54	Processional
55	To Those Who Would Say He Is Unhappy

Part Four

59	Reunion
63	Acknowledgments
65	About Lyman Grant

Old Men on Tuesday Mornings

Part One

Small Bird

I'm slow to recognize the urgent language
of small birds. One morning, sitting at a picnic table
under shadows of El Capitan in West Texas
reading Thomas Merton, I finally awoke
to chirps, gurgles, and squawks of songbirds
in low brush near by. How long had they
been screeching? My awareness gradually unwound
from distant cathedrals and returned to high desert.
I have lost my notes from that day, so I can't
identify the memory birds—Mountain Chickadee,
Bewick's Wren, Virginia's Warbler?—but they were
a noisy bunch as they hopped and leaped among branches
and spikey leaves. Then as they quieted, it emerged,
the Black-Tailed Rattlesnake, their danger now
open where every creature could see. This afternoon,
I eased from Jim Harrison's songs to small gods,
to the racket of jays and warblers in the oak
of my neighbor's yard. My old lesson sluggishly
slithered out of the thickets. Searching for trouble,
I found it twenty-feet up—the buff-breast
of a magnificent hawk. Even from my distance, the feathers
so soft, they looked like fur of a beloved pet.
Tiny birds jumped and fluttered, yelled and shouted,
reminding me of a scene in a movie maybe
I have only imagined. Peaceful citizens, mothers,
shopkeepers, gathering around a lone man
sitting on a park bench, pointing, crying,
"Him, him, beware, that's the man who did
those awful things!" Making right, assigning shame,
a community surviving in its wisdom.
I always wanted to know what a hawk knows.
Today, I watched him uncoil and fly away.

Humanities

For some time I assumed I was changing
the world, a young man in his own classroom

planting seeds of wonder in neglected
gardens of middle-class kids. Now we are

told forty-two percent of college
graduates never read another book.

Teaching literature is a little
like training dogs. You point toward the truth;

they stare at your extended hand, panting,
expecting treats, believing that wisdom

is something they have the nose to sniff for.
With patience, you can teach some to perform

the tricks you were taught. Soon enough we have
circus acts we call universities.

I don't mean to be so nasty, but I
could have done something better with my life.

In traffic today I watched a couple
not talk. Her finger flipped the screen of her

cell, quickly and repeatedly, the way
someone long ago perused beloved books,

scratching for the half-buried memory.
He stared at brake lights and obeyed the law.

So They Say

I made one big mistake long ago.
I did not fall in love with coin-ching
the cash snap of crisp currency,

the exhilaration of ever-rising
numbers on quarterly stock reports,
like roadside altitude markers

climbing the continental divide
that would separate me from low
landers, and, cresting, deliver me

into Rand's golden kingdom. Oops.
Luckily, we sad valley dwellers,
in love with things, and not abstractions

that own them, grasp hammer, spoon,
shovel, or pen and make the world
we live in. On occasion, we look up

at egos touring the skies, bursts
of flames heating their bluster.
Gently they ascend in winds only

they can breach. They smile. We smile.
For we know they float above us
merely on their own hot air.

Outer Banks

Reading poems this winter morning
in our home, still except for shadows,
I enjoy the slow, persistent rhythm

of poetry and sunlight strolling
together across the page.
"That morning on the Outer Banks

long ago." That is all I wrote,
and thought, yesterday before waking
the boys, reminding them about

putting away the cereal, and driving
off to work where I sit at the head
of a long table beneath false

light ensuring the blackened paper
we feed back to the state contains
nothing that it could choke on.

This is the turn, where I mourn
our brief, insubstantial moments
of joy or where I celebrate

the undeserved fullness of my
life's shopping basket. But I'm stopped
out there on the Outer Banks, where

everything begins. The sun first
lifts its head and we hear a voice
say to us...what?

Suspended

Some things are unimaginable,
like the cruel clamp of hunger
in suburbs where pantries overflow
with Lays and Hershey Kisses.
I can't imagine any others.
Outside my window, a tiny
cedar elm leaf grabs my attention,
floating, twirling, midair like a moon
waxing and waning, light, dark, light, dark,
light, dark. I imagine it's threaded
somehow to the branch three feet above
by an invisible filament,
spider's web maybe. But there it spins
and drifts in what I assume are
occasional breezes (because
I am sitting inside knowing
perfectly well how hot it is out
there this August afternoon.) A small
thing, defying the gravity
of everyone's expectations.
Unbelievable. My little
miracle today, like finding Jesus
smiling at me in a potato chip.

Fat Man Olympiad

As I topped the hill in the smallest sprocket,
the set the kids call "granny gear,"
proud I did not give up or give out,
I began to open up on the flats,
winning the imaginary race I was playing
in my own private sports network,
I heard a voice behind me tease,
"Watch out, you're about to be passed
by a seventy-five year old woman."
True to her word, to my left zipped
a biker, fit and beaming, her skin crinkled
like copper crepe, iron-gray hair
cascading from her golden helmet.
And the announcers shouted, "She takes
the lead. She's crushing him." I watched
her legs beat a faster cadence and pull
farther and farther away, while I settled
in my usual pace and let her go.

Following the News

about another plane fallen
into an ocean far away,
one moment a dot
on someone's radar,
a swerve, a mote
curved in virtual air,
and the next a void
filling television screens
worldwide, I sit on the porch
watching smooth arcs
of swallow flight, air space
sliced in violent precision,
beaks mudding a hidden nest,
as if attaching a fist-size
bomb inside the eave
of a luggage compartment.

Wandering and Believing

The big god,
the multi-faced god,
the one you never recognize,
because you look for the god
that looks like you.
That god.
The big god....

Oh, who am I to lecture?
What do I know of that god?
It's nothing like you or me,
I don't imagine.
Why would a god concern itself
with the petty, silly incidents
of a life like mine or yours,
lust and joy and rage and grief.

Drifting through the day
like lost lonely animals,
one day we stop
our wandering because
we find a stranger
who looks nothing

like us, who for no
reason other than love,
offers warm food
and cool water
and a bed where
we can rest.

Survival Tactic

Here I am in the suburbs
reading poems about wilderness.
My gums are sore
where the new partials are rubbing.
I could not live long in the woods.
The wolves would chase me down,
and that would, not even, be history.
Maybe I should turn out the lamp
and quit pretending,
but what good ever came from darkness.
Here I go again tearing pages
from a book to make more light.

The List

How can I go through my day with perfect
peace of mind, then when I lie down for sleep
the one thing I kept submerged bobs up and
breaks calm surface? Like a trout firmly hooked,
guilt wiggles around waiting for a net
that I've again misplaced. Have I told you
I'm a lousy fisherman? I expect
fish instinctively to accept the lure.
I never learned their dark, devious ways
or which currents whispered their secret names.
I'm not talking about fishing, am I?
It's Thursday afternoon and I'm writing
a poem. I could be standing in a stream,
or repairing things on that growing list.
I'm pretty sure someone will pay for this.

Deep End

I want to write a poem about my father, but
my language filter's clogged. As I've become my own
Old Man, I realize that it has been decades since
I have tried to please him. Sure, I was one of those
kids who preened at the edge of a diving board,
the summer sun staining me like a berry, "Look, Dad,
look at me." But when I had emerged from the splash,
he had already walked away. He has been dead
nearly half my life, and longer still since I hoped
that he would turn and, seeing, drench us in light.
This is why I want to write the poem, because,
last night, in a dream, as I baked in the lifeguard
stand, I saw him waving in the deep end, drowning,
and I woke before deciding what to do.

Little Storm

I won't forget you, Little Storm.
What do we become if one
by one the memory stones that line
the path behind us disappear?
We turn around and gaze
upon the open field, the river
carrying everything away, and
in the distance a grove of aspens
quivering in the cool late afternoon
breeze, beautiful, but we are lost,
soaked and not knowing how.

Morning Drive

Would things be any different
if I sat, solitary, on a mountain,
the porch of a log cabin,
and each morning warmed
in the high travels of light
above the long plain,
the expansive hours to middle sky
and the quick descent of day
beneath the forest behind me?

Imagining Paradise

For David Jewell

> I know a guy who is visiting paradise.
> I wish he would write. I'd like to know what it's like
> there. He said he wanted to paint. He said he planned
>
> to wake each golden dawn with two, only two, goals.
> I imagine his sky is very, very blue,
> a blue that's bluer than any blue that's squirted
>
> from tubes. And does the sun every day strike a pose
> it is particularly comfortable in,
> like a lemon lounging in a blue bowl, hanging
>
> there all day above the green mountain never
> rotting? I wish he would write. If I visited
> paradise, I'd at least send home a card or two
>
> saying how I was nervous, clumsy, and afraid
> to reach out, caress the ferns, stiff, like canvass fans,
> or simply to soothe the tip of my finger on
>
> the delicate petals of seductive flowers,
> as if they were soft skin like the inside of thighs,
> and then, well, just a mere bruise would ruin the
>   looking.
>
> Anyway, another day has passed and still no word
> from paradise. The silence hangs in heavy air,
> a swallow paused above a nest of open mouths.

Ghost Story

I told her I didn't believe in ghosts,
and there she went, fading into evening
lifting those pale fingers in half a wave,
a smile like she had just denied a kiss.

And how are we supposed to carry on
through this life that seems so like an open
plain obscured by sharp shrubs and swirling dust?
We watch for water, vultures, a barbed-wire

fence, but the mountains rise in the distance
always a couple more day's ride away.
We old men gather at a campfire, where
that last wild part of us can warm itself.

Our good companion, who is as lonely
and lost as we are, tells us a story
about the wife who loved him more than money.
He says he sometimes sees her ghost out here

when moonlight lies beside him and nudges
him awake. I nod as if I too believed.

Seasons

The writer's bio claims he divides his time
between Montana and Arizona.
How, exactly, does he do that? Will time
remain so cleaved? Like a wheel of cheese,
halved? Or does time leak like a dammed river
with a dozen names. In a poem, the line
is never really broken. Its memory
lives throughout the poem, the hum of tires
still sounding while you pause for meals.
A life is more, or less, than weather.

Fresher Air

For John Herndon

>Reading my friend's new book,
>poems drawn from birds and flowers,
>excised of everything but being
>alive in a world we did not create,
>is like breathing in the old air,
>the air passed from blood and lung
>and leaf and back again
>over and over and over for centuries.

From What Planet

She stands in front of the granite counter
in the kitchen, a knife clasped in her right
hand, the carrots, celery, sweet onion,
hardneck garlic separating, falling
apart at her quick focus. Sunlight wraps
around her from the high windows above,
her strong shoulders still during her cutting,
her back straight and bright. When she turns to smile
at me , the glare of love almost blinds me,
stumbles me backwards into another
room. We have loved each other for nearly
twenty years. Still some days it's as if she
just landed in my life, this familiar
stranger, this alien inspiration.

Cooking

Colleen's downstairs frying meat
in a cast iron skillet and I hear
the sizzle rising through the rooms,
up the staircase, and try to think
what it sounds like. The sloshing
popping, hissing, it doesn't sound
like anything other than what it is.
Fire and flesh. Still I think
about our lovemaking the other
night, both of us shocked, gasping,
terribly surprised by the heat.

Part Two

Ode American

> "It were a vain endeavor,
> Though I should gaze for ever
> On that green light that lingers in the west.
> I may not hope from outward forms to win
> The passion and the life, whose fountains are within."
> —Samuel Taylor Coleridge

1.
A poet walks into a coffee shop
And realizes right away it sounds
Just like the opening line of a joke.
Slightly chagrined he orders a double
Americano and warmed blueberry
Bran muffin. The cashier with long black beard
Smirks at grumpy old man with short gray beard
As if he knew something about time and
Happiness the old man had forgotten.
The poet frowns because he knows *tempus*
Fugits no matter how many *diems*
One *carpes* at the latest hipster bar,
But he will merely prove the barista's
Expression by making the obvious
Point: been there, done that. Finding a table
In slanted light, the poet carefully
Arranges his Moleskin book and fountain pen,
Exhales as if to clear a century's
Decline from his uncollected conscious,
And promptly decapitates the muffin,
Whose scratchy ingredients will ensure
A flow, if not inspirational, then
At least guttural. Haplessly, he waits.

2.
And waits. There is nothing to say except
Today is like another day. The new

Refuses to undo the tedious
Repetition of his somnambulant
Expectations. How can he wake himself
Each duly pleasant morning to the crack
Of joy? Comfort is so habitual.
In his psyche's iPod®, the greatest hits
Of his life's soundtrack is set on replay.
A poet walks into a coffee shop.

3.
This morning, the bused and sparkling tables
Are burdened with optimism's debris,
Push cards, coyly placed in jaunty angles,
Attracting maximum accidental
Interest from the consumer's practiced
Disinterest. Twelve thumbnailed Photoshopped®
Headshots aimed at our un-self-reflexive
Recognition of individual
Inadequacy. *Inspire and Improve*:
Two days, twelve workshops. $500.
Each face beams satisfaction, grins brightly
The unkept secret of success. Sell, sell,
Sell Yourself. No matter the crisis or
The cause, the product of the Conference Class
Is Hope, hope you, too, can be a leader
Possessed by confidence, initiate
Member of the meritocracy of poise.
Happiness spreads from your uncritical
Acceptance that aggrandizement becomes
The How-To Masters, the Fix-It Prophets.

4.
Fork over a Franklin for fresh caffeine
And roughage, account for change, before
Dropping a Washington into the jar.

Another morning gazing at passing
Suits and heels, power's dress code paraded
On downtown sidewalk runways, these models
Of success posing in perpetual
Motion, machines bilking by the quarter
Hour, each step scheduled in some inner
Daily planner. The poet watches these
Name-brand lives pass before his generic
Eyes and dies a little himself before
Recalling Poor Richard's thirteen values.
Jots notes to remember frugality,
Justice, moderation, tranquility.

5.
The poet's mind escapes to a nearby
Park. Between bitter sips, he roves, eyeing
The hopeful: mothers guiding strollers pray
For ancient knowledge women nowadays lack;
The homeless wish for one day without cops'
Batons; the old woman, bowed by years like
A harp, hums a tune that sounds like Gershwin,
While she dances her walker from shadow
To sunlight; a vet with a blown left arm
Balances on one leg and breathes into
His meditation. Enlarge, Enlarge, don't
Blink. The dry stream, where the homeless sleep,
Watered settler's horses; the oaks' massive
Branches shading Apaches roasting autumn
Acorns. Deer, bobcat, fox. Migrating Monarch
Butterflies, Cedar Waxwings, Golden Cheek
Warblers. Great Sea receding, arriving.
Salamanders, oysters, muscles, algae.
Today, the mockingbird cascades his joy,
Pouring over everyone in the park,
Drenching us in celebration. We should

Be prancing, like children, through the sprinklers
Of song, dripping joy's generosity.

6.
Then three or four iPhones® erupt across
The cushioned complacency of the mock
Living room. Ringtones and alarm bells assault
The cheerful harmonies, corporately
Condoned, caustic warnings of impotent
Dangers: Amber's stolen children, wayward
Seniors, timbers blazing, creek beds raging,
Rapture's raising. The gray professional
A table over mouths politely toward
The poet's fluster, "Another shooting."
Our daily dose of penance, a nation's
Tithe for the freedom to protect itself
From itself: possess more guns because we
Own too many guns; kill because we fear
We will be killed. Work and idle moments
Cease while faces screen themselves in horror's
Daily pageant. Mournful anxiety
Drowns out the peppy hit parade until
It morphs into paranoid sympathy;
And soon all that is abnormal resolves
As empathetic congratulation.
We dodged another one. Now, where were we?

7.
Two doors down from the coffee shop, a man
Crouches, knees to chest, folded like a closed
Pocketknife. His downcast face rises, glints
Like a bade opening as the poet
Approaches, but turns toward the suited man,
Shining and fit, gripping his large To-Go

In one hand, folded bills in the other
Extended casually between two
Fingers as if tipping the concierge.
The poet jumps to grab the still open
Door, ponders why he feels he's just been cut.

8.
It's pledge week on the public radio
Station the coffee shop pleasures patrons
With: cough up dollars for news you can muse
To, classical tunes that you can brew,
Dude. For four double *Americanos*
A month, the poet—he is reminded—
Can be membered as sustaining freedom
Of thought, liberal arts, the good life, hope,
The philanthropic way. The cultural/
Social stock exchange at play, Carnegie
For middle-brow stiffs. Survival shifting
Shapes as Maslow may. Music marketed
As meditation, art advertised as
Happiness (like visual cocktails, booze
For ocularly abused), poetry
Promoted as self-improvement (metered
Mysticism for misanthropes). Today
The pledge drive starts. Do your part, the poet
Pleads, abandon commerce, return to Art.

9.
The poet plugs into his own playlist,
That personal mix of philosophical
Admonitions, essential memories,
And meek reminders of beauty's dues.
Old man, beware of darkness, may you stay
Forever young and love one another

Right now. Today it's old tunes heading down
To crossroads, laying down sword and shield,
Catching trains to Macon, singing farewell
To Baby. Patton's watching water rise
And says he'll drive her to the edge of town.
Mississippi John's got the coffee blues,
Goes all the way to Memphis to bring his
Lovin' spoonful home. Nodding in mono,
The poet bleaks his morning by wearing
Other people's blues. Blind Willie McTell
Knows when "a white man go to the river,
Take him a seat and sit down, the blues overtake
Him, he jump and drown." Not me, the poet
Croons. His only trouble is that he has
No trouble. Lord, have mercy, he reflects,
Everything, even grief, is delusion.

10.
One chilled morning, the town is filled with fog
So dense that past and memory captains
The car. As if a character from Twain,
The poet steers the route his knowledge maps
In imagination, expectation
Read and tallied through numbers and colors.
Three streets and right. White headlights blaze passing,
Like barges. Avoid. Safe passage tethered
To taillights, like Alaskan prospectors
In London, stepping into each other's
Prints. Anticipating the coffee shop's
Green sign through mists as if marking a wharf,
A dock, a clean, bright place to contemplate
How present and past splash against the banks
Of the future. He drives ahead with hope
Faint, coffee with cream, *Americano*

Dream, another MacAir® seeking freedom.
Time measured, not in minutes nor hours,
But in refills and language beating toward
The bottom of the page. The poet sips,
Declaring his independence, and writes
A poet walks into a coffee shop
And sits alone. Thus he waits and turns within.

Part Three

Old Men on Tuesday Mornings

Mostly, we talk about our fears, that we'll be forced to be
the kind of men that we would never wish to be. For me:

it's the guy scooting about that motored thing at Safeway,
because my knees and gimpy hip can't bear the weight of my

bad habits. Thank God, I'm still limping along, leaning over
my cart, pushing past the Werther's caramels, the Ensure,

and Depend. Who knows how much time I have before I give
up and become that creepy coot, basket brimmed with lottery

tickets, cheap beer, cheese, and condoms! The last merely for show,
we suppose. Even now, before that dreadful day, we know

that women, including wives, have begun to indicate
disinterest in any dis-ease we could communicate.

Then there is work. Because pay checks have shrunk (like the other
parts), one of us worries his lucrative career will come

full circle, forcing him to take, again, the measly job
he jettisoned so proudly when the gravity of youth

gave way and he entered the orbit of adult success.
What will become of us, we fret, now that our contact lists,

like our backs, have begun to weaken? Which will give out first,
our pensions or our pride? But we laugh. Our fears, unruly

pets, are locked away in kennels of possible
futures. We take them out for walks and water breaks. Perhaps

a shit. Our conversations are plastic bags we pick up
worries with. So we keep talking. Hey, we've survived this long.

Heirlooms

When they were younger, the husband
could not understand why his wife,
whom he had married for hidden

skills and absent inhibitions,
always insisted on pruning
the wild, rangy heirloom roses

he'd shamelessly planted along
the front walk as his personal,
yet private, congratulations

that his house, more than his neighbors',
was where extravagant beauty bloomed.
His wife cut them short, almost flat

to the ground. She had her reasons,
which he had never understood.
They grew back wilder and fiercer

she said. The same applied to hair,
but she never cut hers that short,
except once, that last time, years ago.

I see that old man now each spring
out front clearing up the tangle,
cutting back all his knotty trunks

to the ground. He has his reasons.
And we neighbors luxuriate
in his tidy extravagance.

With Time

He keeps hunting for something new
that will remind him of old joys,

a flint, a spark, a match, that ignites
the debris swept in the corner

of a higher room in his brain.
He scrolls Itunes for his lost desire

to dance or howl or seduce. He
lurks around the borders of the "*Times*

Best Sellers List" for peeks into
another's secrets that he could steal.

On the tube, no new answers to old
questions: it's still good guys and bad

guys, except bad guys win. Hopelessness
dazzles its special effect. He still

plays his guitar like a beginner.
Sometimes he thinks he has become

a mound of moldy leaves. The best
he'll do is smolder, reek a cloud

of smoke too low to catch the wind.
Give him time, he'll rot. With patience,

something he's learn of late, he'll return,
perhaps, as part of something green.

Bio

You walk into a room and stop
because you can't remember why
you went there. Are you lost or are
you where you always planned to be?

No one blames the rangy pumpkin
vine for its wild, unruly life.
One day a seed breaks open. Greeny
desire squirms through darkness toward

the light. Hope—or is it something
violent like anger, greed, fate—
forces itself into and through
a crack, an ache, an imperfection.

Some God pours someone else's shit
upon you, and you find a way
to discover the good in it.
The vine grows where it can. The sun

changes its place far, far away,
all day, every single day,
yet the vine never stops. It roots
for a time, and moves on. Then all

these beautiful blossoms emerge,
delicate things. Look what happens
to them. They morph into tough nubs,
ugly fleshy failures, while you

keep urging ahead unaware
that behind you those shameful
false starts have grown large, succulent,
the objects of celebration.

Wherever you go, it's a new
room. You ask yourself "where am I?"
All you know is where you've been,
and all the effort left behind.

At Eighty-four

If he could, he would die driving
his tractor, shoving limbs and brush
from this pile to that, and grinding
the low gear, lifting full buckets
forward, just so. He's completed
the big projects, pond digging, dam
building. There's nothing left to do
there but gaze, blue herons on one
leg in the whispers of cattails,
glass surface rippled by turtle rise.
He yanks the rope of his chainsaw,
delights in its bite and smoke, and
each season extends his ladder
to reach a higher, distant branch.
The women in his life scold him,
predict a gnawing, gushing fall.
Today, he douses the big mound
with diesel. The roar and rise of flame.

Lab Work

It's not the practiced joy
of the phlebotomist
it's not the whiff
punch of alcohol
wipes cleaning the skin
it's not the snap
of the rubber tourniquet
strangling the forearm
it's not the tap tap tap
on the median cubital vein
disturbing one's morning
like an unsolicited sales call
it's not prick pain
of the needle penetrating
or the fist releasing
it's the gray and the frail
in the waiting room
the old man shuffling in
too weak to lift his legs
scooting his swollen feet
as if dragging two chains
that soon would reach their end
it's his gnarled smile
and knotted hand raised
to another set of strangers
it's his practiced arm
laid out like a dancer's,
ready

Last Rights for a Family Man

Let's say you have five minutes.
What cold secrets will you confess?
Your addiction to sweets while you
drive around, doing errands, filling

your fat cheeks with Hot Tamales?
The lies you spread about the co-worker
who stood on the rung right above you?
That joke he told really wasn't racist

but your boss need not know that,
now. But you could never admit
those few dates with the girl, barely
legal, who believed she was free

and wild, and thought two afternoons
in bed with you was just the chain
to yank to wake her dull parents
to her silent desperation.

Your assigned role is to provide
the bitter, rigid example. Still
we all have treasure chests buried
on far away isles and casks filled

with stolen joys floating far off
the reefs of our respectable lives.
Yes, everyone is a pirate, secret
outlaw, thief, and we all know

the smiling hypocrite gripping
the scorecard operating his own
personal guillotine, gallows, electric
chair, waiting for us to confess.

Shame and the Silent Moon

You want to say something to the innocent one
whose eyes opened large and wide as if her uncle

had offered the wrong gift when you kissed her beneath
the moon that long ago spring. You thought you were wild

and wise about the world you were conquering.
But now it all seems like wine splashed by a careless

and cocky hand upon a white table cloth. Where is
she? What could you say? What good is apology

now that you are an old man, a second round
of children gathering on Sunday afternoons?

Maybe, you hope, she remembers the moonlight
and a tender hand at her waist? Maybe, she was

not really a child and you weren't merely a wolf
and her lips weren't enflamed with fear, and bruised.

Clear Stream

The old guy sometimes imagines that he
could live out in the country. A sturdy
cabin near a clear stream. Bags of coffee
and sacks of beans. Cold bins of potatoes.
Some independent chickens. A random
collection of wisdom books and mysteries.
Such thoughts, like weeds, invade the tended lawn
of his retirement on summer mornings
when his wife is shopping or afternoons
when she's away visiting their children
in neighboring towns. He brews a pitcher
of iced sweet tea, the old fashioned way—
with loose leaves and white sugar. Nabs a couple
of gingersnaps from the resealable
bag. Sits in his parents' favorite wingback
chair in the freshly vacuumed carpeted
living room, accented with framed posters
from Rothko retrospectives at the Met.
He reads a book on romanticism,
written by a mid-century scholar
who wrote, it seemed, as if he respected
his reader. The country and a cabin,
that could be his life—a little closer
to the hawks and the wolves. Yes, sure, it could.

Hot and Sour

So he's wasted the week, ill and quick-tempered.
Good news passed over him like satellites, distant
and unrecognized, while bad news, even minor annoyances,
rampaged like hungry wolves, snarling, cornering him
defenseless on the couch with only his remote to distract them.
In France, another crazy man revved greater revolutions of death.
At home, fascists spread like kudzu, and AK's sold as well
as Bibles. Flex Seal will repair the bullet holes, this week
two for the price of one. And the man, sexually abused
as a teen, qualified to go to Las Vegas on *American Ninja
Warrior*, but the Alaskan Inuit fell from the I-Beam Cross.
When will this fever—as endless as primary season—break?
When will the antibiotics begin to work like Raid, and when
will his wife return home with that Hot and Sour Soup?

Guarding

He is prepared. Two kick boards, flippers, hand
paddles, pull buoys, earplugs, nose plugs, goggles,
silicone cap. On mornings when he swims,
he arranges it all at pool's edge, and
stretches the ache away. He stands alone
to face a pool whose depths and distances
he's begun to dread. Water shimmers, late
summer breeze and shifting light. The surface—
oak trees a hundred years old, maybe more—
becomes a skim of shadow and sparkle.
The limestone pool house upends and reclines,
a sheen of paled color, insubstantial,
and lays the image of the locked iron gate
for him to leap himself through. Almost half
a century ago, he stood gearless
and fearless by similar pools, mostly
for girls, and the rare opportunity
to save another's life. Now it's his life
he guards, a mile at a time, back and forth,
back and forth, making clumsy turns, smoothing
strokes, strengthening kicks, counting
laps, ticking off the days, always leaving,
always returning, always disturbing
the undulating surface of his own
reflecting, approaching, departing, and
approaching the shimmering locked iron gate.

Family Pride

You can devote your entire life
chasing the person you always
hoped to be, like a devoted
lover stalking his beloved,
only to discover once you
move very close, her tiny hand
gently hovering over yours
on a family holiday,
that no one particularly
likes your imagined better self
that is materializing
finally right before their eyes.
You are a habit they refuse
to let you break, a mirror
reflecting nothing of the selves
that they will not themselves become.

Affluence: Still Life

    The bowl of fruit poses center table.
    Like a stag in open meadow, you think,
    and your eyes narrow as if taking aim.
    You're hungry. You're empty. Go ahead. Grab
    the apple and bite into it. Take large
    violent bites until juices cascade
    down your chin, until you've reduced that red
    beautiful fruit, with streaks of pink, cloud-like
    patches of cream, reduced that fruit to core,
    the seeds revealing themselves, like frightened
    fawn. And those you swallow, too. Was that enough?
    Or will you now clutch the bunch of grapes, yank
    them from stem, roll them around on tongue
    until you clamp down that animal jaw,
    grind them into pulp, gulp down the sugars?
    How long can this go on? How much ripeness
    can one person desire? Pears, mangos, plums.
    take it all. Or maybe you could merely
    sit and leave the abundance to someone
    else, poised, glowing in sunlight, and you, still,
    hungry, knowing there will always be more.

Success

He reached a point where he really didn't care.
He thought it was his greatest achievement
to come to the place in which he could
walk through the chilled slaughterhouse of life
and avoid the hooks that dangled there
ready to hang him up with someone else's
fears and desires. Anxieties flew about
like splattered blood—that was unavoidable.
It had taken years, decades, half his life
to learn to keep his head. Then, as he became
respectable, the money stable, and the kids
enabled into beings more or less self-sustaining,
like birds, rehabilitated, released into the wild,
he discovered he missed his old story,
the doubt and hunger, the fearful fang and claw.

Open Carry

You don't want to stare
but your eyes keep slicing his way.
Then your raised chin aims
your buddies' attention to the guy
at the counter and the weapon
holstered against his lumbar.
You weren't afraid, but now
your body begins somehow
to nudge you from the inside.
Never have you feared of terrorists
or desperate seekers of oxy or meth
in this second Tuesday's La Madeleine
until this cowboy entered.
Stirring your black bitter
with a couple of regular Joes,
now the hackles spike as if you were
a pack of dogs lazing about the yard
licking and scratching
and shooting merely the breeze
when suddenly a wolf saunters in
all strut and insult to your canine sloth.
Your ironic smile about an article
in the *Times* or something Brzezinski
and Scarborough implied this morning
about Trump begins to arch
into a snarl and an unpracticed growl
rumbles deep inside your chest.
Another white guy with a gun.
The cartridges of memory spin
until you see yourself through
the sights of some old western,
meek farmer come to town
to swap stories and trade for sundries
the wife has been wishing for.
But the vigilantes are thirsty

Lyman Grant

for revenge, whenever any is called for.
So you apologize to your friends,
say today you need to get home early.
Still you decide to carry proudly, openly,
for the dark stranger to see, your box
of rich surprises with its pink bow,
your butter croissant and Sacher torte parfait.

Waffle House

The old man
in the booth said,
"Now I have arrived
where I am,
I wish I had paid
better attention,"
grinding the cigarette
stub into a saucer,
jabbing his fork
into the slice
of American cheese
laid out warmly
upon his grits.
Then he reached
for the syrup,
sticky
and somehow
artificial.

Arroyo Sunset

Evenings, the two sat on the porch
watching the disappearance of time.
One knew more than the other
the darkness that rises inside,
then rushes forth, uncontrolled,
like May floods in a dry land,
the roar and debris bursting
beyond the banks of otherwise
peaceful and gentle waters.
One wished to rise and walk
out past the fence line, just to see.
The other held out a hand,
"Let's just look from here this night."

Here They Are

The congregation raises their faces
toward God abundant with joy,
like silver salvers overflowing
with cash and welcome cards,
their eyes glistening like loose change.
They plead, so fully, so loudly,
before communion "Send me, send me,
Lord," then bow their heads, and remain
seated for the closing prayer.

Mountain Prayer

What is one to do when hunters pack off
into mountains and you are left behind
to tend to summer fields? From your window
you keep seeing a white dove ascending
and disappearing into nearby trees.
God has funny ways of making our most
dangerous adventures the most boring.
Fall asleep and you will not die, you will
simply never awake. Maybe the dove
is building its nest up there. Remember
the air in the forest, saturated
vanilla, the ground layered in faded
copper needles, the rare sign of something
wild. Around the campfire, after stories
and laugher, silence speaks its truer faith
in the waning moon. Forget the dove. If
you listen, that silence drifts all the way
down here where still there's plenty work for you.

Processional

The rain today clambering on the roof
before you begin your big adventure.

Out windows to the east, there is no sun,
but day begins all the same.

Nothing is as you had planned.
So you sit and heave and begin

to grow little disasters in your heart.
Look at the surprises God has brought.

Still, you have known men
who delivered little bouquets of joy

even as they trudged through mud.
As they pass by, why not join them?

To Those Who Would Say He Is Unhappy

He would wish you to know
that he wakes each morning
just like you, pleased
that he has beaten the alarm,
tickled by that last blink of night.
The day lays itself out before him
like a great runway that he taxis
awaiting take off.
Today, like every other day,
he expects to be a rehearsal,
a tour, another practice session,
before returning to the hanger.

He will relish the usual pleasures,
the sticky juice of a peach wetting
his whiskers, the giggle of a yet
another generation, the ignition
bite of his restored high school
Chevy Bel Air, the whisky warm
chest, John Wayne wobbling
unholstered into another saloon.

One day, he knows, when the attendants
say buckle up, they will mean it.
No need for return fare.
So it is not unhappiness you see.
It's a deeper kind of contentment,
the blind fish in the lowest pool
of the darkest cave
who knows the joy of dawn
without light.

Part Four

Reunion

For the 1971 Temple High School Senior Class

    Tonight, did you stand in the open door,
    Hesitant, and scan the room
    Like you did the first class
    The first day of high school,
    Searching for the friendly face,
    Someone's eyes to sparkle in recognition,
    A nod that allowed the doors of an anxious present
    To open to the sunlight of a friend-filled past
    Look, we saved a seat for you.

        You are not alone

    Each of us wonders if we will be remembered
    For the dropped pass in the fourth quarter,
    Or the stupid gesture we made in the class photo
    Where we imagine everyone's eyes still stop
    Dismayed and offended,
    That gap in our knowledge that prompted
    The wave of giggles across the classroom
    Until it splashed upon the teacher's face
    And wiggled there like a beached fish.

    Does anyone know how far and how hard
    The road has been just to get us here?

        You are not alone

    Like contestants in a television competition
    Challenging our talents, endurance, and our fears,
    One by one, we step from behind the curtain
    Of our private daily trials into this late stage
    Of our present lives and are welcomed here
    By each others' applause.

>We made it this far
>We are not alone

Yes, some of us should lose weight.
Some of us should stop smoking.
Some of us must keep working a few years more.
Some of us found AA.
Some of us still have unrealized dreams.
Some of us create new dreams every day.
Some of us ache for a lost child.
Some of us grieve a spouse.
Some of us made one big mistake long ago.
Some of us have been washed in underserved love.
Some of us did not make it this far
    and still they are here in memory's unclosed book.
Some of us found God.
Some of us walked away.
Some of us see the world half empty.
Some of us hold cups overflowing.
Some of us survive accidents and illness, disease and indescribable
    discomforts.
Some of us still dance in spite of it all.
Some of us still rock and roll.

>We are not alone

There stands the friend who helped you master geometry,
And there the guy who got you the lifeguard job at the country club.
There's the boy or girl you always wanted to kiss.
That old friend helped you with that big curl in your hair for prom.
Remember the time you laughed so hard with those girls
    you peed in the front seat of your car and that made everyone laugh
    louder.
And those boys stuffed fruits in their brassieres.
That girl's favorite song was "Ain't No Mountain High Enough."

Those boys smoked pot and listened to *Atom Heart Mother*.
She was the science wiz and added ions or something in her head.
He sat next to you in typing class and always beat
    you by five words per minute. It was infuriating .
Isn't that one of the guys who made the principal curse at the pep rally?
That gray haired man once looked like a Beach Boy.
That composed and mature woman is the goddess
    in the white bathing suit you fell in love with one summer.
That smiling man really is the boy with the best personality.

        You are not alone

We are grateful you stepped through that door.
If you wish tell us where you've been
Or where you hope to go.
The evening's young and we've only just begun.

Acknowledgments

Some poems have previously appeared in print and on-line journals:

Aliens (Raw Paw), *Blue Hole, Chicon Street, Concho River Review, Di-Verse-City, Enigmatist, Illya's Honey, In Between Hangovers, Red River Review, Poetry at Round Top, Texas Poetry Calendar, Visions International*, and *Voices de la Luna*.

About Lyman Grant

Lyman Grant has taught composition, literature, humanities, and creative writing at Austin Community College since 1978. He has also served in various administrative roles, including department chair of creative writing, dean of arts and humanities, and dean of communications. He has published poems, essays, and reviews in many periodicals and anthologies, including *The Dallas Morning News*; *The Texas Humanist*; *Texas Observer*; *Texas Books in Review*; *descant*; *Concho River Review*; *Sulphur River Literary Review*; *Feeding the Crow*; *Literary Austin*; *Is This Forever, or What?*; *Big Land, Big, Sky, Big Hair*; *The Beatest State in the Union*; and *The Great American Wise Ass Anthology*. From 1989-1992, he was the editor of *MAN! Magazine*. *Old Men on Tuesday Mornings* is his fifth book of poems.

www.ingramcontent.com/pod-product-compliance
Lightning Source LLC
Chambersburg PA
CBHW021449080526
44588CB00009B/761